Don't you just hate that?

Don't you just hate that?

738 Annoying Things

by Scott Cohen

Workman Publishing · New York

Library of Congress Cataloging-in-Publication data is available.

ISBN 0-7611-3321-6

Design by Paul Hanson and Elizabeth Johnsboen

Workman books are available at special discounts when purchased in
bulk for premiums and sales promotions as well as for fund-raising or
educational use. Special editions or book excerpts can also be created
to specification. For details, contact the Special Sales Director at the
address below.

Workman Publishing Company, Inc.
708 Broadway
New York, NY 10003-9555
www.workman.com

Printed in United States of America

First printing March 2004

10 9 8 7 6 5 4 3 2

*To my mother
and father,
a lifelong source of
inspiration*

Acknowledgments

I would like to thank the following:

Family: Jay and Phyllis Cohen—no parents try harder. My sister, Randi Bennett, and my brother, Mitch Cohen—always my biggest allies. My sister-in-law, Suzanne Cohen, for always baking; my brother-in-law, Lloyd Bennett, for always paying. The Bennett and Haimowitz families. My nieces, Jennifer, Melissa, and Samantha—sorry for not dedicating the book to you—and my nephews, Spencer, Ryan, and Kyle, for understanding the value of a good pile-on.

Book people: My editor, Richard Rosen, who improved pretty much every point and kept me laughing the whole way through. My agent, Rick Diamond—without your help I'd still be e-mailing this book to my friends. Thanks to Rebecca Schiff and Sophie Deutsch for helping solicit the lists of professional annoyances, and to the anonymous irritable people who wrote them. Thanks to Janet Pawson.

Friends: (from shortest to tallest): Larry Dobrow, Gia Hochstein, Tami Smiler, Johanna Skier, Jessica Hemmerdinger, Donna Estreicher, Beth Werfel, Tammy Marks, Patty Dwyer, Laura Brounstein, Robin Busch, Stephanie Buchstein, Olivia Hayward, Fran Bolanis, Beth Amsel, Eric Salpeter, Donny Hochstein, Jon Schwartz, Craig Buchstein, John Krasno, Danny Werfel, Jeff Skier, Ricardo Diaz, James Rosen, Eric Samansky, Eric Schleifer, Sara Rosen, George Bolanis, Mark Hemmerdinger, and Greg Laub.

Also: Bill Hanjorgiris, Thurman Scott (THANK YOU), Meredith Finnen, Robert Egan, Marie and Frankie Jilling, and everyone at work and 71 Irving.

Don't you just hate that?

1. Wondering if the appetizer you're sharing with a friend is being divided evenly.

2. Having to make that face to people in the hallway at work that implies "Hey."

3. That Barry Manilow didn't write his hit song "I Write the Songs."

4. Restaurants with indistinct figures, like a rooster and a chicken, indicating which restrooms are for men and which are for women.

5. That 41 seems to be the average age of people who describe themselves as in their "late 30s" in personal ads.

6. Walking by the same person you've already walked by in the dairy, produce, and frozen-food sections.

7. That it takes a blackout to get most New Yorkers to say "hello" to one another.

8. Believing, as a squirrel looks directly into your eyes, that it is looking into your soul, when in fact it is trying to determine whether you have any nuts to give it.

9. When you try on a garment in a store and think, I wish I could wear this—and then think, I can, I can wear this. So you buy it, and never wear it.

10. Being yelled at in a foreign language in a foreign country.

11. That the student who warns his classmates not to make it a popularity contest when voting for class president almost always loses the election.

12. Apartment buildings that don't have a thirteenth floor because of superstitious people.

14. That your requirements in a mate become stricter as you grow older, and your good looks wane, making it harder to attract even the mediocre people you no longer find acceptable.

15. The tiny percentage of General Tso's chicken–eating Americans who know that Tso was in fact an utterly ruthless man.

16. Watching a movie with your parents that shows full frontal nudity.

17. Realizing how good the water pressure in your shower was, now that you live in Cuba.

18. What the "About the Author" on a book jacket doesn't tell you (e.g., "In addition, Lawrence has not called his grown children in seven years").

19. That it would be socially unacceptable, at your age, to wrap a Fruit Roll-Up around your pinky and suck on it for two hours.

20. That Maine is never chosen over Vegas for bachelor parties.

21. When your nieces and nephews reach the age where they can distinguish a cheap gift from a valuable one.

22. That nailing a triple lutz in the Olympic Figure Skating Finals is one of many joys you will never know.

23. Finding a rusty AA battery, old packets of mild Taco Bell sauce, and a picture of your aunt and uncle tossing a Frisbee, as you frantically search your glove compartment for your registration while the state trooper grows impatient.

24. That both Simon and Garfunkel went bald.

25. Having to preface the majority of what you say with, "I can't recall if I've mentioned this to you before, but . . ." because you can't remember what you've told to which of the two people you're dating.

26. Feeling guilty for not socializing with the owners of the bed-and-breakfast you're staying at.

27. When a woman calls out "Thanks a million!" and waves as her car pulls away, and you realize that you just gave her totally wrong directions.

28. When your childhood friend who was always better than you at everything is still better than you at everything.

29. That, thanks to man's pioneering spirit, Mt. Everest is littered with empty oxygen canisters.

30. Politicians who believe that any economic problem can be cured by opening a casino.

31. The tiny percentage of times that a song dedication played on the radio is actually heard by the person it's being dedicated to.

32. Wondering, having applied 20 SPF sunscreen, then a layer of 40 an hour later, whether they average out to 30, add up to 60, or if it's only the last layer of 40 that counts.

33. That nursery school is just another forum for bullies.

34. When the most engaging human interaction of your day is answering "Rolls" to the question "Would you like your stamps on sheets or in rolls?"

35. An open parenthesis that is never closed (like this

36. The feeling you get when you clip your nail too far.

37. Having something valid to interject into the conversation of two nearby strangers, but knowing that society does not permit you to do so.

38. Being unable to forget someone you spent three minutes with 11 years ago.

39. Trying to trick the public by waiting and waiting . . . and then wiping your wet palms on your pants after a messy sneeze.

40. Yoga instructors who smoke.

41. That men reach their sexual prime at 19, and women reach their sexual prime at 33—but it's far more common to see a 33-year-old man with a 19-year-old woman.

42. That by the time most people have saved enough money to travel the world, they are too old to endure such a trip.

43. When a Staples opens next door to your new business, 3-Hole Punch.

44. Recalling the tactless things you said at the wake.

45. That bands named after a city, state, or continent are usually lame (e.g., Asia, Kansas, Alabama, Europe, Chicago, Boston, America, Berlin).

46. When your thigh rubs against a leather chair, emitting a loud, ripping noise, and every time you rub your leg against it again, in an attempt to make the same noise to prove to the public that it wasn't a fart, it sounds nothing like the initial noise.

47. When your fringe friend doesn't realize that you're trying to remove him from your life.

48. When you're paying for something at a store and they ask you what ZIP Code you live in.

49. Parents who refuse to believe the negative things teachers say about their children at parent-teacher conferences.

50. When the driver pushes the unlock button, but you pull the handle at the same moment, and remain locked out.

51. Feeling like an idiot when you realize how common the word is that you couldn't think of.

52. Not being malicious enough to want to see your ex live unhappily, but not being bighearted enough to want your ex to live free of regret.

53. That despite the overwhelming evidence to the contrary, the myth that hammocks are comfortable for napping somehow endures.

54. Friends who view karaoke as their chance to shine.

55. Enduring a caning from a vicious prep school headmaster in New England in 1925.

56. When you've waited so long to send a gift that sending one now would be more offensive than not.

57. Pets that only show affection right before mealtime.

58. The momentary frenzy that ensues the instant that a cashier calls out, "This register is now open."

59. The moment you realize that "braving the hurricane" wasn't a wise idea.

60. Jobs where they try to make you feel better about your salary by giving you a meaningless title like Assistant Director of Postage.

5 Annoying Things About Being a Woman Working in a Men's Maximum-Security Prison—*by A.L.*

1. That Kevin was offered three packs of cigarettes by another inmate if he would introduce me to him.

2. That a prison is full of men who notice when you get a haircut.

3. When, as part of a preparole career preparation course, I ask the class to complete sample job applications, and one student asks, regarding the conviction question, "How do you spell 'hijack'?"

4. When your most well-received class, "Grammar in the Slammer," is discontinued for bureaucratic reasons.

5. When an inmate tells me: "Aw, you don't need a boyfriend. You've got 2,300 boyfriends *right here.*"

61. The stunning speed with which marriage can destroy a lifelong friendship.

62. TABLE 5:

Hank & Eve
Jeffrey & Johanna
Lenny & Tamara
Jonathan & Kathy
Robin

63. That the song "Take This Job and Shove It" failed to show the poverty that the fellow endured later in life.

64. When the brief thrill of making the yellow light ends and you're bored again.

65. When your only memory of your Sweet 16 is projectile vomiting on the DJ's arm.

66. Therapists who feign interest by nodding and occasionally asking, "And why do you think that is?"

67. The lingering suspicion, each time you lather up with "2-in-1 shampoo plus conditioner," that it isn't quite as effective as applying shampoo and conditioner separately.

68. Remembering enough French from high school to know that the two Frenchmen sitting next to you are talking about you, but not knowing enough French to understand what they're saying.

69. When you've accidentally broken something in someone's home, and the host doesn't try to comfort you by saying, "Oh, it was already broken" or "It does that all the time."

70. People who exaggerate the danger of picking up a piece of broken glass.

71. Being the last person on a long line that no one else seems to be getting on.

72. That people who tell you to "give it 110 percent" rarely go beyond 83 percent.

73. When the person you are waving hello to doesn't see you waving, but then catches you awkwardly retracting the wave.

74. That it's the people who can least afford to lose their money who play Lotto religiously.

75. Feeling that you might fall through every time you step on a metal grate, despite the enormous likelihood that you won't.

76. When a stranger asks you for the time, and your fear that you won't be able to answer in an appropriate time span causes you to blurt out, "9:17. No, 10:17! No! 9:17!"

77. When a friend says "I have good news for you!" and it concerns her.

78. The slow, insidious way that your love for something is sucked out of you when you do it for a living.

79. People who consider dropping cigarette butts on the sidewalk "acceptable littering."

80. Knowing that a dime has 118 ridges around its edge, yet not knowing where your great-grandparents originated.

81. Wedding toasts that end up being more about the person giving the toast than the bride and groom.

82. The slow admission to yourself over a period of years that you'll never have a good body.

83. When seeing men who are less attractive than you dating women who are more attractive than the women you date doesn't give you hope, but instead leads you to wonder what's wrong with your personality.

84. Finding an old "To Do" list, most of which remains undone.

85. Realizing that "I'm sure I'll see you around" really means "I'll make no effort to meet you, but perhaps we'll run into each other by accident."

86. When your house is inadvertently listed on a star map as Anna Kournikova's.

87. Return envelopes that treat you like a moron ("Did you enclose your check?" "Did you sign your check?").

88. When your dad sings the chorus of "Penny Lane" as "And Elaine is in my ears and in my eyes."

89. When you thank the cashier for packing your groceries but your attempt at brightening her day elicits no discernible reaction.

90. That future generations will look back on the early 2000s as an era in which we did nothing but look back at the 1970s and '80s.

91. When your babysitter is too busy talking on the phone with her boyfriend to play with you.

92. When you're giving your credit card number over the phone and the person says "Uh-huh" after the first few numbers, so you say the next bunch and pause, but there's silence—and the moment you begin saying the next number she says, "Uh-huh."

93. Feeling neurotic for patting the grease off your pizza with a napkin.

94. Not being able to throw out an old magazine because it has an article you want to read that you know you're never going to read.

95. Getting a Q at the end of a Scrabble game when all the U's and blank pieces are gone.

96. When someone asks, "What's up?" and you reply "I'm fine, thanks" because you assumed he'd ask "How are you?"

97. The fake road scenery that whizzes past drivers in old movies.

98. Listening to your accountant reiterate the tax advantages of losing all your money in the stock market.

99. Carrying an item you own into a store that sells that item.

100. Wondering if the guy who prepared your meal is the same guy who scribbled SHOVE IT! on the sign that reads EMPLOYEES MUST WASH HANDS AFTER USING REST ROOM.

101. Celebrity impersonators who don't give up the bit offstage.

102. Orange juice being sold with "No Pulp," "Some Pulp," and "A Lot of Pulp," when what you really crave is "Between No and Some Pulp."

6 Annoying Things About Being a School Nurse—*by G.F.*

1. Head lice, because they don't make the kids sick, they just make the parents crazy.

2. That because of the President's Council on Physical Fitness, all of the middle school kids have to go running, even though I know some of them are out of shape and they'll come back injured and unable to breathe.

3. Lower-school teachers who send children to the nurse for a paper cut that I can't even find.

4. That students take condoms and I find them later all over the school, filled with water.

5. Teachers who panic over a nosebleed and forget to give the kid a tissue, causing him to bleed all the way to the office.

6. Girls who fake their period to skip swimming.

103. The teacher you had as a kid who thought his "tough but fair" routine would make you look back on him with gratitude, but whom you still remember as a small-minded tyrant.

104. When your girlfriend, who is sitting on your lap, asks you if she's crushing your legs, and she is.

105. That only when space aliens attack our planet will we stop killing each other (we'll focus on killing the aliens).

106. Receiving a birthday card in the mail eight days before your birthday.

107. Trying to convince yourself that batting seventh in the lineup somehow speaks to your strengths as a hitter.

108. The amount of mayonnaise most delis put in their tuna.

109. Dear Mom,

I really hate camp. I have no friends, and everyone teases me because I can't swim. I want to come home.

—Dylan

110. Never knowing whether to call it "seltzer," "club soda," or "sparkling water."

111. Stumbling over something in front of strangers and immediately having to decide between two options: (a) ignore your misstep and try to

walk nonchalantly onward;
or (b) look over your
shoulder while making
a slightly exaggerated
look of annoyance at the
thing that caused you to
stumble, as if to imply
"They really ought to
fix that!"

112. When your car gently taps the back of someone else's and the other driver makes a big production out of "checking for damage."

113. Listening to someone who doesn't know how to play piano play piano.

114. Tipping someone who hasn't earned it only because you don't want to look cheap.

115. When you e-mail a friend and he responds to everything except the question that addresses his deepest insecurity (e.g., How was the party

Saturday night? Did Beth show up? Are you still going through with the liposuction?).

116. Sharing a long car ride with a dull acquaintance who doesn't feel comfortable with silence.

117. When all you want is to be fired so you can collect unemployment, and you can't even accomplish that.

118. When you sign the back of your new credit card and it looks nothing like your signature.

119. Biting your cheek on the swollen area where you've previously bitten it.

120. Being unable to keep the kite aloft, while your child sits in the grass, quietly weeping.

121. Sprinting to your car at the end of a day's work—because you're a scab.

122. When the waiter asks "Is everything all right here?" right after you've taken a big bite of your sandwich, causing you to grunt your response.

123. Being the only one who hasn't reached puberty, when the coach shouts, "Great practice! Now let's hit the showers!"

124. Spending every New Year's Eve with your one friend, who is also perpetually single.

125. That nobody who asks you to "lower it just a tad" really wants you to lower it by only a tad.

126. Our mission statement (and the steps we'll take to achieve it): The dispersion of solar rays through meandering tubes manufactured by the Scandinavia-based Zwantzen Group, insofar as the Zwantzen Group can remain solvent while maintaining a national telemarketing campaign aimed at inundating the American public with phone calls, disturbing in both their content and delivery, and unleashing a wave of e-mails with subliminal subject headers that confuse the public into opening these e-mails, thus exposing them to our report about solar ray tubes. If the marketing campaign fails, then Fritz Estreicher, vice president of the Zwantzen Group, will fund and manage the creation of nine new casinos in Salt Lake City to lure the Mormons into gambling religiously until, unbeknownst to them, they've lost their money and houses, the proceeds of which will be reinvested into a third marketing wave, targeting stay-at-home, Oprah-watching moms, explaining why it is vital to their future and their children's future and their children's children's future, as well as the legacy of their parents, grandparents, and great-grandparents, that they support the spread of solar ray tube distribution throughout our country. It is vital that the telemarketers explain that the cancer-causing solar tubes are going to be manufactured and stored in Scandinavia, not in New Jersey, which the American public will logically assume.

127. College students who believe hallucinogenic mushrooms aren't harmful "because they're natural."

128. The people exercising in a gym who look at you through the window, making you feel flabby and worthless.

129. How Lincoln Logs fool children into believing that it's easy to build a log cabin.

130. People who cite group characteristics about an ethnic group, but in a positive way (e.g., "Koreans are really industrious people!").

131. When the sprinkler jams, flooding a small patch of grass surrounding it.

132. A television weatherman gesturing in front of a huge map of the United States and hollering about barometric pressure, when all you want to see is the five-day forecast.

133. Not liking the gift you pulled out of the grab bag as much as the one you put into it.

134. When you hold the ketchup bottle over your french fries and the first thing that comes out is red water.

135. Listening to a detailed explanation of how to do something you already know how to do.

136. The armrest warfare that takes place when two stockbrokers sit next to each other on an airplane.

137. Late fees for a video you didn't have time to watch.

138. What most skateboarders amount to.

139. In this movie Joe Pesci plays a short-tempered short person.

140. Hating yourself for resenting the old lady who takes forever to serve you at the doughnut shop.

141. That your close friend's decision to get married will cost you $50 for the engagement party gift, $100 for the bachelor party or shower,

$120 to rent a tuxedo or $220 to buy a dress and shoes you'll never wear again, $150 for the gift, $400 for airfare if they're having it in Vermont, and suddenly you've blown close to $1,000.

142. People who are afraid to step on an escalator . . . missed it . . . how 'bout this one . . . no, not that one . . . wait, not that one, either . . . *that one*—no, not that one!

143. Tornadoes that don't kill the people who chase them.

144. Sushi snobs who frown upon people who order shrimp shumai dumplings.

145. When all your husband wants to do during the third day of your honeymoon is stay in the hotel room and watch the NFL draft on ESPN.

146. People who point at their wrist while asking for the time.

147. Every time you try to focus on the positive, the fact that you can't find a job interferes.

148. Not knowing what "def" means.

149. Listening to the repulsive sound of your voice leaving a message on your friend's answering machine as she plays her messages in front of you.

150. That bacon will never be considered a vegetable.

151. The fact that "a good idea, if well executed, will outperform a great idea that is poorly executed" means little to you when you're someone who never has ideas.

152. That it's the ones who love you who are most adept at tormenting you.

153. When your kids agree that "only a racist would say that," and you think, Gosh, that's one of my favorite expressions.

154. Realizing you left a porno video in your parents' VCR as you stow your carry-on luggage in the overhead compartment.

155. Hating the fact that you always say "muah!" while kissing everyone hello.

156. Never being able to remember the difference between a chimichanga, an enchilada, and a quesadilla.

157. When your reply to a question depends on your complete comprehension of a word you don't know.

158. Remembering how people of your current age seemed so old when you were a child.

10 Annoying Things About Being a Comedian/Comedy Writer—*by M.M.*

1. Seeing a line you wrote show up on throw pillows, pot holders, and greeting cards in whimsical gift catalogs.

2. When the comedian who goes on before you covers all the same areas you are planning to cover, but with better punch lines.

3. When family members who have always had doubts that you were funny are sitting in the front row.

4. When the comedian who goes on before you does raunchy sex and bodily excretion material, and you must follow with your droll remarks about the presidential hopefuls.

5. When the celebrity who is the centerpiece and punch line of your best joke is suddenly the victim of a tragic illness or accident.

6. When the person about whom you have written hilarious, vicious jokes is seated in the audience . . .

7. . . . and your former spouse, on a date, is sitting right behind him.

8. Having the bartender decide to blend a new batch of margaritas in the middle of a delicate joke setup.

9. When your best joke makes a high-profile appearance on late-night television without you.

10. When, after all the time and work you put into thinking up new material, someone gets a large advance to write a book full of lists by other people.

159. Only being able to complete the tedious tasks you've been putting off when you have a more pressing chore to tend to.

160. When your car has one of those pathetically high-pitched horns that implies: "It's okay, you can step all over me."

161. A sneeze that lingers in your nose, and then absorbs into your forehead.

162. Realizing that your favorite part of any event—the office Christmas party, taking your kids to the amusement park—is the food.

163. Public restroom sinks with separate faucets for hot and cold water, forcing you to choose between ice-cold and scalding-hot.

164. That your last moment of unqualified glory was in Little League 31 years ago.

165. When a piece of cheese falls into a crevice between your refrigerator and the counter, causing you to spend the next few months wondering what is happening to it.

166. The unfortunate unfashionability of earmuffs.

167. One-hour commute
x 2 commutes per day
x 5 workdays per week
= 10 hours commuting
per week. Ten hours of
commuting per week
x 50 weeks = 500 hours
commuting per year.
Five hundred hours
commuting per year x
45 years = 22,500 hours,

or 2.57 years of your life spent commuting.

168. That pharmacies don't have a "Staff Recommends" section (e.g., "Fruit-Eze Stool Softener is my favorite. Perfect consistency." —Harold).

169. When a moment of serenity reveals how crazed your life normally is.

170. Realizing after several attempts that you've been trying to insert a three-prong plug into a two-prong outlet.

171. When your mom calls you by your corny childhood nickname in front of your friends (e.g., "Hey, Chipwich!").

172. Rubbing your palm over the tiles as you search for the light switch in a public rest room.

173. When the one thing you have a passion for is destroying your health.

174. When lice lay larvae in your daughter's hair.

175. Banana bruises that aren't visible on the outside of the peel.

176. Sensing that your opponent is more interested in physically harming you than winning.

177. That perfecting doo-wop harmonies with your buddies on street corners is really not an option for you when you live in the mountains.

178. When your lies multiply faster than you can remember them.

179. All-cap e-mails (e.g., BECKY: MAKE SURE YOU ALERT SARAH THAT RAPHY'S GROUP WILL BE ARRIVING AT 9:40. DITTO FOR BEN. —RICHARD).

180. That "I'm sorry, Zoe, the batteries were not included" is not an acceptable answer to your four-year-old daughter.

181. People who don't remove their Christmas decorations until March.

182. That celebrities who are fairly new to their fame often consult more-established celebrities for advice on how to handle celebrity, and that you belong to neither of these groups.

183. When the closest you come to achieving your dream of having a pool in your backyard is the plastic kiddie pool filled with brown water by the side of your house.

184. When your father tells a long, meandering joke to the waitress who is holding a heavy tray, then mistakes her obligatory laugh for a real one.

185. Being antibacteria but also anti-antibacterial soap.

186. When a homely person compliments you on your looks, forcing you either to return the compliment insincerely or say thanks without saying anything more, thereby removing any doubt that you don't find him attractive.

187. That it's no longer acceptable for sailors to skip down the street whistling show tunes.

188. When even a passing stranger can look at the two of you and tell that your relationship is failing.

189. Accidentally setting your alarm clock for P.M. instead of A.M.

190. When missing the bus by 20 seconds plunges you into a deep trench of self-reproach.

191. That "Saturday, Saturday, *Saturday*. Saturday, Saturday, *Saturday*. Saturday, Saturday, *Saturday night's all right*" is copyrighted.

192. Wondering, based on his answers, if the person you're copying from knows less than you.

193. When your husband, who still clings to his '60s leftist ideals, feels the need to strike up a meaningful conversation with every custodian, gas station attendant, and busboy.

194. When the car driving behind you has a ski rack attached to the top, making it look like a police car in your rearview mirror.

195. That plastic surgeons earn a lot more than pediatricians.

196. People who have no clue how loudly they talk.

197. When your lover's cat jumps on the bed and seethes whenever the two of you become intimate.

198. Skipping work the one day your boss doesn't show up.

199. That you can't wear leather pants convincingly.

200. That the greatest expression of love most people receive is at their funeral.

201. People who insist that celery has no taste.

202. Musicians who go by one name that's a common noun (e.g., Sting, Jewel, Seal, Brandy, Edge).

203. Realizing, while trying to beat your kid in Chutes and Ladders, that you are the competitive creep you've always been accused of being.

204. That during their life span, the average American falls 738 times more than they fall in love.

205. That you're the only one who'll never see what you look like while you sleep in public.

206. When someone tells you to "Have a good weekend!" on a Thursday.

207. Overhearing someone whisper "Who is that clown?" as you walk into a party.

208. When an audience claps to a song out of rhythm.

209. Waiting for the pain to arrive in your toe the moment after you've stubbed it into the leg of a chair.

210. Pinball machines that only give you three balls.

211. People who emit the "heenh!" sound while trying to hold in a sneeze.

212. Wondering if the person who used ".." meant "." or "...".

213. That almost nobody scrolls through microfiche anymore.

214. Wondering whether the best gasoline is 87 (the cheapest), 91 (gets the best mileage), or 89 (neither the most expensive nor gets the worst mileage).

215. How no one ever says "Hi, Dad" into the camera.

216. Being convinced that everyone named Amy is part of a vile race of mousy aliens sent here from a very mean place.

217. That no one will ever care to distinguish between your "early work" and your "later periods."

218. The smell of burnt hair.

219. Recalling the misery that we put our substitute teachers through.

220. When your doctor asks if you mind if an intern watches your colonoscopy.

221. Knowing that service people at certain national retail chains ask "How are you today?" only because company policy forces them to do so.

222. Seeing the nonessential things in your wife's bag as you struggle to close the zipper.

223. The liquid at the top of a Dannon yogurt.

224. Driving by a stranded car with someone sitting in it on the side of the highway, knowing that one day, sooner or later, that will be you.

225. Wondering if your boyfriend's pattern of ordering the second-cheapest bottle of wine is coincidental.

226. That the days when "I don't know" was an acceptable answer as to why you did something stupid are gone.

6 Annoying Things About Being a Feature Film Casting Director

—*by E.L. and J.T.*

1. When a director or producer tells you that her daughter doesn't think an actor is cute enough.

2. Auditioning actors who, after shaking your hand with a sweaty palm, tell you they have the flu.

3. Being called a casting *agent*.

4. When your relatives ask you why you cast a particular actor, whom they hated in the movie.

5. When actors take it too far in auditions by vigorously miming their physical actions, like pretending to urinate or drive a car.

6. When actors tell you a little too much about their personal lives.

227. People whose contributions to legal discussions consist of things like "He oughta fry!"

228. When your child asks you to explain why water spurts out of the faucet when you twist the knobs.

229. People who leave their laundry in the machine for hours, yet get angry when you remove it.

230. When, after a hefty meal, an abrasive friend of your parents slaps you on the back and says, "Boy, you can really pack it in, eh?"

231. Occasionally feeling guilty because your grandmother allows you to live in her house rent-free and you use her basement to manufacture and sell bootlegged movies on DVD.

232. The way your body feels the morning after playing football with your friends, who are also over 40.

233. Amusement park fatigue.

234. Applying the postage so you can mail in the payment for your speeding ticket.

235. The myth that scaring the crap out of someone can eliminate their hiccups.

236. Being slowed down by a 35-cent tollbooth.

237. When nothing brings you as much joy as criticizing other people's work.

238. The myth that a rubber band can blind someone.

239. The second-to-last day of a vacation.

240. That *Anna Karenina* sits on your bookshelf, while you continue plowing through John Grisham novels.

241. When your kid wears a glove throughout the ball game and your seats are in the most remote part of the upper deck, where it is physically impossible for a foul ball to reach.

242. The vulnerability you feel while sitting on a public toilet.

243. Accidentally e-mailing to "All" when you meant to reply only to "Sender," creating a lifelong rift between two of your closest friends.

244. Being unable to twist a jar open and unwilling to let someone else give it a try.

245. When your Caller ID reveals that the terrifying stalker calls you're getting are coming from your own home.

246. The average human falls asleep in only 14 minutes. Many people who read this statistic tend to ponder it each night in bed, making it more difficult for them to fall asleep.

247. Injecting needless spite into family situations.

248. That no one can explain the purpose of a silent letter.

249. Having to examine a map publicly in a foreign country.

250. People who rationalize "I'm a better person for it" after every negative experience, despite the fact that you are never a better person for having lost your wallet.

251. Men who drink diet soda.

252. That the psychology establishment's rate of discovering new mental disorders interferes with your ability to enjoy the ones you have.

253. That those guys combing beaches with metal detectors never actually find anything.

254. When the agony of turning 40 makes you ashamed of how depressed you felt on your 30th birthday.

255. Disgusting feet in sandals.

256. An acidic vomit burp.

257. Men who automatically associate any kind of physical affection with sex.

258. Watching someone in spandex jogging at 7 A.M. as you stumble home from your all-night drinking episode.

259. When your six-year-old daughter asks you 23 minutes into the flight to Australia, "Are we almost there yet?"

260. Concentrating so hard during a standardized exam that you can't understand what you're reading.

261. When you first started dating, you found it cute that he enjoys hunting elk and you prefer creating mosaic tile designs, but now it's not so funny that you have little in common with your husband.

262. When you refrain from mocking a professional athlete only because you fear that he'll jump into the stands and pummel you.

263. That at 10:27 A.M. you're already starting to think about where to go for lunch.

264. The odds of your being there when Springsteen or Van Morrison hops on stage at some local club.

265. How the commercialization of Christmas forces Jews to give more expensive gifts for Hanukkah.

266. Irish films in which every word sounds like "shite."

267. That the inventor of the spork is a wealthy man, while Eric Schleifer, inventor of the foon, lives in his mother's attic in Fort Wayne, Indiana.

268. When someone says on your answering machine, "Tag. You're it!"

269. When the button you push on your remote control doesn't respond at first, and you push it again and get channel 33 when you wanted 3.

270. Eating a turkey sub alone in your apartment on Thanksgiving Day.

271. Trying to act astonished and flattered while entering your surprise party, which you already knew about.

272. Kissing hello the people you would never have invited to your surprise party.

273. Burger King's slogan "Have It Your Way," when we all know they manipulate us into ordering one of four basic combo options.

274. Jogging with a friend who keeps a faster pace.

275. Wondering how to convey to the well-meaning woman on the train, who has just said "Cheer up," the extent to which your life has just fallen apart.

276. When your car is the only one on the block that doesn't have a NO RADIO IN CAR sign hanging in the window.

277. That every time you come to accept your current level of hair loss, there's a more profound stage awaiting you.

278. That if aliens abducted you and returned you to earth radically enlightened, no one would believe you, and whatever you could contribute to the sum of mankind's knowledge would be completely ignored.

279. An offer that pops up every time you go online, forcing you to click either "Yes, I'd like to order now" or "Not now, perhaps later."

280. A tiny dog angrily barking at a huge dog as if it could kick its ass.

281. When the person you're eating with aggressively wipes his mouth with a napkin, causing you to wonder if he's hinting that you have a glob of something dangling from the corner of your mouth.

282. Having to gush over every aspect of your friend's new home (e.g., "Oh, the wooden knobs on these kitchen cabinets are *adorable*!").

283. When the subtitles in a movie are the same color as the background.

284. Feeling guilty for giving your sister the bamboo vegetable steamer your Secret Santa gave you.

285. How uncomfortable white people feel when black people call each other "nigga."

6 Annoying Things About Being a Starbucks Barista—*by A.N.*

1. People who try to pronounce "croissant" with a French accent.

2. Customers who ask for "a regular coffee."

3. People who are talking on the cell phone when it's their turn to order, then resent it when I skip to the next person in line.

4. Yuppies who think they're adventurous for ordering lattes with flavor shots.

5. People who call us to reserve a bagel.

6. Escorting customers to the rest room and unlocking the door 56 times a day.

286. That it's impossible to ask someone how he likes his meal without it being interpreted as a hint that you'd like a taste.

287. Wading through a large, motionless group of people.

288. The enormous mental anguish children inflict upon one another.

289. Being one of the two birds being killed with one stone.

290. That the "sober you" is never as much fun as the "blacked-out you."

291. When your trip to Paris makes you realize how tasteless the rolls are at your hometown bakery.

292. Not knowing what to do with yourself every Tuesday night from 8:00 to 9:00 now that your favorite show is off the air.

293. When you introduce yourself to a stranger and she responds, "Sure, I know you. We've met a bunch of times!"

294. That Jack LaLanne in his nineties can bench-press more than you.

295. DJs who, as a song ends, thoughtfully repeat its most clichéd line as if it's profound.

296. People who figure that getting married will reduce the sting of their partner's aggravating habits.

297. Trying to find a sincere Mother's Day card that isn't too sentimental.

298. That every time you try to impart wisdom to your teenage son, he replies *"Duh!"* without lifting his eyes from his Game Boy.

299. Cutesy product names that misuse the letter Z (e.g., "Cheez," "E-ZPass").

300. When your hosts can hear your urine splashing into the toilet because the bathroom has no fan and is adjacent to the dining room.

301. The contempt the other magicians show toward you because you reveal how the tricks are done.

302. Having your first bargaining offer accepted, leaving you to wonder whether you could have done better.

303. A brochure tucked onto your windshield that looks like a parking ticket from across the street.

304. When your spouse tells two of the same three stories whenever you go out to eat with another couple.

305. People who stop telling a story "because it's too disgusting to tell during dinner," leaving you to try to envision what was so disgusting about it as you continue eating.

306. How air blasts out of a tire as you connect the pump to inflate it.

307. That all of the library pencils need sharpening, but the pencils at Off-Track Betting write with remarkable efficiency.

308. When your 14-year-old is more sexually active than you.

309. The vicelike grip that a select group of men holds on the world's riches.

310. How painful a pimple is when it's located directly below your nostril.

311. Wondering if your students find social studies as tedious as you do.

312. That the FCC allows television commercials to be as loud as the loudest part of any television program.

313. That courting a woman nowadays entails sending a few e-mails and perhaps an Instant Message.

314. That the delicious smell of gasoline is unhealthy yet there's nothing unhealthy about breathing in fecal fumes.

315. How nauseating the fifth mozzarella stick or pancake tastes.

316. When you ask a telephone rep to take you off their mailing list and he replies, "No problem. You may receive our catalog for the next four months while our computer processes your request."

317. Stretching a rubber band to its limit in an attempt to get it around something, but still falling a millimeter short.

318. Waking from a dream in which you were a coward, proving to yourself that you are one both consciously and subconsciously.

319. Wondering if your ex, whom you're still obsessing over, has forgotten you as quickly as you've forgotten all of your other exes.

320. Not wanting to do something, but not wanting to not do it.

321. Blowing $125 on some long-past-his-prime performer, then spending the car ride home convincing yourself that you didn't get ripped off, with thoughts like, Oh, he really puts on some show.

322. When you first learn that there is no Santa Claus, and realize it's only one of the many lies you've been told.

323. When you yell "Has anyone seen my wallet?" and your spouse calls out "It's wherever you left it, honey."

324. When your three-year-old mimics everything your five-year-old does, and currently, your five-year-old is stabbing your stereo speakers with a fork.

325. Learning the hard way that "lesbo" is not an appropriate word.

326. When your co-workers resent you because you've been voted "Employee of the Month" two months in a row.

327. That you like the "whoosh" sound made when someone swings a pool cue around in a menacing manner.

328. When every thought, each micro-movement of your fingers, is focused on an inane act, like bending a deformed paper clip back into shape.

329. The barrage of irritating sounds you endure each day.

330. Noticing that you answered True for nine of the ten questions on a True or False exam, and wondering whether any test would ever have that high a percentage of Trues.

331. What you'll find in the average American garage.

332. "Attention, Bedding Essentials shoppers. It is now 8:15. Bedding Essentials will be closing at 9:00. Please make your selections accordingly."

333. Jukeboxes that only have greatest hits compact discs.

334. Discovering an area of talent that will never be of any benefit to you (e.g., being able to speak backwards fluently).

335. Forgetting in which situations "which" is supposed to be used instead of "that."

336. Potato chip companies noting that "Contents may settle" on the bag, 90 percent of which is filled with air.

337. People who strategically place their bag and jacket on the seats surrounding them so no one can sit there.

5 Annoying Things About Being a Hairstylist—*by L.V.*

1. People who ask me to do what I want and cut as much as I want, then say it's too short when I only cut off an inch.

2. When clients decide they are going to highlight their own hair with Jolen Creme Bleach the day before they have to attend a wedding, and then proceed to freak out when you can't fit them in for an emergency six-hour color correction.

3. Clients who constantly touch their hair or move around in order to make eye contact with you during their cut.

4. People who tell you how they want you to hold their hair as you cut it, and which scissors to use. Hey, I'm the one who paid for Beauty School.

5. When clients show me a picture of Heidi Klum and ask to look like her when they are five feet tall and have superkinky, damaged hair.

338. When your diet strategy consists of taking in as much NutraSweet and nicotine as possible.

339. A blood clot under your fingernail that is visible for 13 months.

340. Preachy vegetarians.

341. Trying to avoid eye contact with the guy at the urinal next to you, as he tries to do the same.

342. When you can't remember the initial topic of conversation—which was far more engaging than the one you're stuck on now.

343. Those moments when your life depends on getting $2,500 in cash, any kind of vehicle you can get your hands on, and a fake passport.

344. The difference between the scenes in the travel brochure and your vacations.

345. That mankind hasn't figured out how to harness the obsessive anxiety of planning a wedding into a viable energy source.

346. Becoming nauseous from eating too much raw cookie dough.

347. People who keep their clock set 10 minutes fast "in case I need the extra time."

348. Any movie preview that begins, "In a time where darkness reigned supreme and heroes were few . . ."

349. When someone wins the $48 million lotto and claims "it won't affect my lifestyle."

350. White guys with a Snoop Dog cell phone ring.

351. When all your Cracker Jacks have melted into one big Jack.

352. Knowing that you'll never again be a child who can fall asleep in the backseat, feeling completely safe while your parents drive you home.

353. Having no clue when to use a semicolon.

354. Losing track of time in the diner's restroom and coming out to find everyone huddled under the counter, gagged and bound.

355. Rearranging heavy furniture, then realizing you liked it better before.

356. That even animal rights activists couldn't care less what scientists do to rats.

357. Knowing that your friend who screens her calls is probably listening as you leave a message.

358. That we use words like "testicle" and "vagina" to describe genitalia, and wonder why so many English-speaking people have issues with sex.

359. People who don't pronounce the letter H (e.g., "Their house was euge!").

360. When your heart skips a beat, reminding you of its eventual failure.

361. Putting an I SUPPORT THE LOCAL POLICE sticker on your car, as if that will save you from getting a ticket.

362. When the first 45 minutes of a one-hour meeting is spent recapitulating the previous day's meeting.

363. Feeling so bored during retirement you actually miss the job you hated.

364. That every movie taking place in the late '60s must contain music by one of the following bands: The Doors, Jefferson Airplane, Steppenwolf, Three Dog Night, or Creedence Clearwater Revival.

365. Gas tanks that are empty the moment the needle points to EMPTY.

366. The futility of going back to sleep in an attempt to finish a great dream.

367. Trying to establish that you're not a lowlife after bouncing a check.

368. When the maître d'
approaches you and asks,
"Just one?"

369. When your fear of
forgetting a vital piece of
information forces you to
repeat it in your mind:
"Don't forget the passports,
don't forget the passports,
don't forget . . ."

370. People who are not your relatives who send photos of their child at three months, six months, nine months . . .

371. Realizing you were wearing the same outfit the last time you hung out with this person.

372. The taste of a fortune cookie.

373. When a teacher erases the entire blackboard but misses one prominent chalk mark.

374. In this movie Tom Cruise plays a feisty, can-do type of guy.

375. Having constantly to assert your heterosexuality because of your lack of success with the opposite sex.

376. When The Eagles' "The Best of My Love" gives you unsettling flashbacks to your dentist's reception area.

377. "Wet hair. Shampoo. Wash. Rinse. Repeat."

378. When everyone in the room is feverish with NCAA "March Madness," and all you can think about is some minor task you forgot to take care of at work.

379. Child guards on lighters and aspirin containers that make you feel like an imbecile.

380. When the woman you're courting admits to being unable to resist men who are competitive kayakers.

381. People who hide their money under the Monopoly board.

382. When your Seeing Eye dog goes blind.

383. Sensing it was Satan, not nature or nurture, that shaped you.

384. Watching the era you grew up in turn from the recent past to retro to history.

385. When the D.A. asks what you meant when you wrote in an e-mail: "Graft is a beautiful thing."

386. Receiving parenting advice from someone you don't respect.

387. Stoking the fire for your girlfriend at the ski chalet and ending up with a room full of smoke.

388. Having an acute anal itch in public.

389. The cop who's pissed tonight.

390. Realizing the company softball game is going to be a lighthearted affair instead of a competitive game in which you could finally prove what a stud athlete you are.

391. When your kids reach the age where they can spell "I-C-E C-R-E-A-M" and "B-E-D-T-I-M-E."

392. When you see veins and gray things inside the chicken nugget you tore open.

393. The perverse pleasure we get from watching home videos of natural disasters.

394. Watching the band at your bar mitzvah on its break, as they wolf down food at a little table in the back.

395. Realizing, as your body submerges during your first scuba dive, that you're still not over your claustrophobia.

396. Needing to pay someone to help you pay your taxes.

397. Lunatics whose lunacy is only discernible after you've married them.

398. The stench of the cheese section in fancy food stores.

399. Wondering if your brother, who just bought a 40-foot yacht, is shallow.

400. The tedious process of removing a piece that you accidentally dropped into the wrong slot while playing Connect Four.

401. Sensing that your Ryder truck might not fit under the overpass.

402. When you meet your girlfriend's friends for the first time and know, as you get up to use the restroom, that they'll be talking about you the whole time.

403. When you give the right answer during class and your teacher responds "Good for you," which you and your classmates decipher as "Congratulations, doofus, you finally got one right."

404. When your eyes instinctively dart to the side because the man sitting across the aisle caught you staring at him, heightening your urge to look one last time. So you slowly pan your eyes back, only to be caught again, further intensifying both your desire to peek again and your fear of getting caught a third time.

405. Wondering if you are entitled to the deep sense of loss you feel when a celebrity you admire dies.

406. When "Purple Drizzle" is the most original song you've ever written.

407. After waiting 28 minutes to see your doctor, a nurse brings you to a room—where you wait another 28 minutes.

7 Annoying Things About Being a Personal Trainer—*by K.M.*

1. When a client pulls at a microscopic piece of flab on her thigh and asks, "What exercise can I do to get rid of this one little squidge right here?"

2. People who come here with really, really offensive BO or extreme perfume.

3. Guys who pick a bench and sit and read a newspaper for twenty minutes.

4. "You know, I'm in really good shape even though I haven't been to the gym in over two years."

5. People who sing along to their Walkman.

6. People who think they're cool because they sweat a lot.

7. Guys who get all territorial about machines.

408. Any menu item described as "gently nestled."

409. Suspecting that your son keeps making so many errors in Little League because you broke in his glove improperly.

410. Wondering to yourself, "Do I really listen to music that loud?" every time you start your car.

411. The moment between dry heaves when you realize another heave is coming.

412. When everyone is congratulating you on achieving something, and only you know that your achievement was obtained fraudulently.

413. Politicians who frequently begin sentences with "frankly" or "in all candor."

414. That Valentine's Day was placed in February—just in case single people have recovered from the loneliness that Christmas and New Year's Eve induced.

415. When they put a scoop of ice cream on top of your cone but none in it.

416. That no one knows anyone who has finished James Joyce's classic *A Portrait of the Artist as a Young Man.*

417. When a radio station only comes in if you stand frozen in an absurd position.

418. Getting arrested for successfully climbing to the top of a huge building.

419. Feeling guilty as your bags pass through the airport's X-ray machine despite the fact that jaywalking is the most illegal act you've ever committed.

420. That houseguests often come in waves.

421. Waking up from a two-hour nap at 10:18 P.M.

422. That even the fanciest restaurants suffer from pest-control problems.

423. Reading "Unable to extricate himself from beneath a boulder, a man severed his arm with a pocketknife and walked 20 miles to safety" and thinking, The closest I've ever come to that was when I clipped a hangnail from my thumb and walked 20 steps to the refrigerator.

424. The level of humiliation Monkey in the Middle can cause.

425. Delusional people who only wear army fatigues.

426. Having to make up the work you missed while you were out sick, but never getting a chance to make up the fun you would have had if you weren't sick throughout the weekend.

427. When your boyfriend promises to cook you a romantic dinner—but when you get to his place, he comes to the door obviously having just awakened and mutters something about the two of you making a quick run to the supermarket "and maybe doing some stir-fry."

428. Wondering who was rude enough to leave an empty roll of toilet paper and then remembering it was you.

429. When your dog keeps cutting from the left side of your body to the right and back again, forcing you to constantly transfer the leash from one hand to the other.

430. Taking the alternate route the radio traffic reporter suggests, only to find everyone else doing it.

431. The strands of dead skin that hang from the roof of your mouth after you've scorched it eating microwaved pizza.

432. Being taught that A.D. stands for "After Death," when in fact it means after the birth of Jesus Christ.

433. How useful the Internet is for stalkers.

434. Hearing your father slur over the phone from Atlantic City, "First I'm up, then I'm even, then I'm down a little. Then I'm down a little more. Bing, bang, boom—next thing you know, I'm twenty grand in the stink'n hole!"

435. When everyone knows that the only reason you weren't the last one picked is that your best friend is one of the captains.

436. Having second thoughts about your first tattoo.

437. When the first sip of orange juice reminds you that you've recently brushed your teeth.

438. When the only shameful thing you've ever done shows up first under a Google search of your name.

439. When a stranger continues sniffling every few seconds but doesn't blow his nose.

440. Inarticulate sports announcers who only get that job because they are famous retired athletes.

441. That you've never been sure what a "Yankee Doodle Dandy" is.

442. Rationalizing that having your heart broken again will finally allow you to get over the first person who broke it.

443.

444. Having to accept 443 for what it is.

445. Noticing the unusually large number of strangers crowding around and staring at you as the stretcher you're lying on is lifted into an ambulance.

446. That someone thinks you're dumb enough to feel pleased that you only spent $99.99 instead of $100.

447. Scrupulously recycling, only to catch the recyclable and nonrecyclable trash being dumped into the same bin.

448. How dull Corn Flakes taste when you're used to Frosted Flakes.

449. The heavy-handed way movie characters are introduced to the audience (e.g., "Lucy, is that your younger sister, Isabel?").

450. Thank-you notes from babies. E.g.:

Dear Aunt Gia,

Thank you so much for the Dr. Seuss books. I've been enjoying them thoroughly and I can't wait 'til I'm old enough to read them. It was so thoughtful of you

and I'm so looking forward
to seeing you in June.

Lots of hugs,

Annie

451. People who think
the entire restaurant staff
is there to serve them.

452. Losing your "over-under" bet because a coach decided to kick a meaningless field goal with three seconds left in the game.

453. Realizing that strangers watched you trying to push open a door that reads PULL.

454. Owning an introverted dog.

455. Trying not to think about what you're thinking about.

456. Not feeling free to patronize your favorite store because of the fight you had with the owner.

457. The humiliation that comes from hundreds of cars slowing down so they can watch the cop giving you the ticket.

458. When your favorite book becomes a movie and you can't find a copy without Tobey Maguire's face on the cover.

459. Teachers who give "pop quizzes."

460. Students who study "in case we get a pop quiz!"

461. The lack of rehearsing that occurs at a wedding rehearsal dinner.

462. Socks that lose their elasticity.

463. Looking at yourself in the mirror on the morning of the day on which you are fated to get into a car accident, and having no idea what awaits you.

464. When your parents, in order to boost your self-esteem, convince you that you're a gifted soccer player.

465. How Muzak manages to extract the few remaining shards of soul that still exist in already lifeless songs.

466. Construction workers who get paid with your tax money to hold a STOP sign all day.

467. When your wife admits in marriage counseling that the mole on the back of your neck has revolted her for 19 years.

5 Annoying Things About Being a Voice-Over Artist—*by H.P.*

1. When I put the headphones on for the first time and they're all sweaty.

2. Trying to make prescription drugs' side effects sound attractive.

3. Having to manufacture a cute chuckle on cue for a diaper wipe commercial.

4. When the client says "That was perfect," and they record it 50 more times "just to be safe."

5. When you're recording something that you thought was important and everyone in the booth, including the recording engineer, is eating lunch and paying no attention.

468. How little a postcard says.

469. When you go out of your way to let someone cut into your lane and he doesn't wave thanks.

470. Waking up with your arm numb and thinking, This time it's paralyzed.

471. The waiter whose slow service forces you to eat like an animal to get back to the office on time.

472. Trying to abort an automated message by pressing # and hearing "That is not a proper entry," then cheerfully, "Goodbye!"

473. Distant relatives you see at the same holiday function once a year, every year, with whom you pretend to have a real relationship.

474. Gas pumps that say PLEASE DON'T TOP OFF on the handle.

475. The stage of a relationship where you and your companion don't feel comfortable not having sex.

476. Getting rope burns on your wrists from playing tetherball.

477. Tipping a bartender for handing you a bottle of beer, but giving nothing to the guy who pumps your gas in the pouring rain.

478. That we judge balding men by the choices they make in coping with their baldness.

479. When you're forced to pick up a second telephone and the person in your left ear says "Huh?" when you respond to the question that the person in your right ear asked.

480. When the smell of an indoor pool brings on a rush of extremely painful memories.

481. When your five-year-old grandson teaches you how to use your new DVD player.

482. When the digital sign above a highway reads NORMAL TRAFFIC CONDITIONS as you sit in bumper-to-bumper traffic.

483. A bumper sticker reading I AM TOO BLESSED TO BE STRESSED.

484. When it finally dawns on you that your 27-year-old son has been a full-time gangster for the past eight years.

485. Wondering if a recent injury that hasn't healed fully will linger for the rest of your life.

486. Regretting getting your kid a pet chicken.

487. When there are a lot of mosquitoes and you're not sure whether to say "I'm going to put Off on" or "I'm going to put on Off."

488. When your mother raises you to always respect your elders and your father raises you to give your respect only to those who have earned it, leaving you uncertain how to respond to the nun who taunts you during class.

489. High fives that don't quite come off right.

490. Receiving 75 cents change, none of which is in quarters.

491. That nobody notices all of the extra care you take to make them comfortable.

492. The criminal feeling you get while sneaking six shirts into the fitting room because they have a "five-item limit."

493. The white thread your vacuum won't pick up no matter how many times you run over it.

494. When you're at a coffee shop and a guy asks you, "Can you watch my stuff while I use the bathroom?" and you say "Sure" and return to reading your book, and when he comes back his jacket is gone.

495. Americans who use British expressions like calling soccer "football" or warning you to "mind the gap" as you're stepping off a train.

496. Overhearing Dad entertaining party guests with the story of how he caught you masturbating.

497. That you aren't supposed to touch a halogen lightbulb while inserting it.

498. People who wave their hand in front of your face while you're peacefully staring into space.

499. That nearly every murderer, pedophile, torturer, extortionist, and rapist is a man.

500. When neither of you is attracted to the other, yet you continue removing each other's clothing.

501. Finding the mail addressed to the prior tenant more interesting than your own.

502. When your grandfather looks like Wilford Brimley with a mullet.

503. That anxiety over a pregnancy scare can cause a woman to get her period later than normal.

504. That there's no way to apply a computer's "undo" function to our personal lives.

505. Being the last person to stop applauding.

506. That finding your roach traps empty only adds to your fear that they don't work instead of reassuring you that you don't have roaches anymore.

507. The way your breath smells after drinking milk and keeping your mouth closed for two hours.

508. That it's no longer considered cool to get stoned in the woods and paint ZEP RULES on large rocks.

509. In this romantic comedy, Hugh Grant plays a sensitive Englishman who gets the girl in the end.

510. When someone tells you that you don't take criticism well and you truly know they're wrong.

511. Stuttering while leaving a message on the answering machine of the one person you want to be romantically involved with.

512. Laughing out loud at the movie you went to see alone.

513. That all good things come to an end, but some mediocre things seem to last a very long time.

514. Not being able to look the woman who cleans your hotel room in the eye because of the mess you left her.

515. Three years into your marriage, your husband's gut really starts taking off.

516. That nearly every square inch of Manhattan has been urinated on at one time or another.

517. When your wish, as you blow out the candles, is that this be the last birthday you spend with the people around you.

518. That you don't have the cash to fly on a moment's notice to Japan to bid on Paul's Sgt. Pepper uniform.

519. People who attach deep significance to their moronic tattoos (e.g., "The fire-breathing gargoyles on my shoulder represent my disdain for organized religion.").

520. The smell of the circus.

521. People who hold a door open for you when you're 20 feet away, causing you to walk faster.

522. That some women use *Sex and the City* as a barometer for how to behave in a relationship.

523. The strain of maintaining that Grandma is the endlessly benevolent person your kids believe her to be and not the manipulative bully you know her to be.

524. That pancakes aren't considered a dessert.

525. When movie characters make out after sleeping all night and not brushing their teeth.

526. When empty ice-cube trays are the only things you can find in your freezer.

527. Remembering the days when people told you that you looked good—and meant it.

528. Feeling uncomfortable telling someone that she has food wedged between her front teeth, yet being unable to avert your gaze from it.

529. Knowing that you succeeded by identifying and exploiting people's weaknesses.

530. People who watch TV news and interpret what they see as evidence that we need to bring on the final race war.

531. Not being able to name one event that occurred between 1067 and 1491.

532. Nodding off during your drug trial.

533. The petty bickering that goes on at your synagogue.

534. In this movie, Michael Douglas plays a well-dressed man caught in a terrifying web of sex and deceit.

535. Personalized license plates that tell you the driver's occupation (e.g., ED CPA).

5 Annoying Things About Being a Company's I.T. Person—*by J.A.*

1. When I've tried everything I know to fix a computer problem and I beg my supervisor to come, and he taps about two keys and the problem is fixed.

2. When, in order to show my supervisor what's wrong, I go through the steps to make the problem happen again and it doesn't happen.

3. When a coworker has a computer problem and as soon as I get there I know they've already restarted the computer, so the problem is no longer there. But when I ask them if they restarted the computer, they look at me innocently, and say, "Huh? I didn't do anything! I didn't restart it, I haven't touched it since the problem happened."

4. When a coworker stops me in the hallway as I'm on my way home (finally) and asks me to help him with a problem because it will only take five minutes, as if I've got the word "sucker" written on my forehead.

5. Fixing the computer of the person who flagged me down after 5 P.M., and hearing him say, "Okay, I'm calling it a day. I really appreciate your help. See you tomorrow."

536. When all the ranch hands openly snicker at you, even though you own the place.

537. Being involved in an unfair fistfight.

538. Channeling your frustration into a wild burst of consumerism.

539. The number of phone numbers you need to remember over the course of your lifetime.

540. Six-foot-tall women who wear high heels to ensure that people of normal height feel inadequate.

541. People whose credo is "Healthy shmealthy."

542. Gray, three-month-old snow piled up by the side of the road.

543. People who say as their food arrives "Oh, there's no way I can finish all of that," and they do.

544. When your well-to-do 60-year-old aunt refuses to date men her age because, "all they're looking for is a nurse with a purse."

545. Having a strong physical attraction to a cartoon character.

546. Cults that build up huge arsenals, refuse to pay taxes, and complain that the FBI is watching over them.

547. Old novels that use odd expressions (e.g., "I know the answer!" Billy ejaculated from his seat.).

548. When your shoelace rips far from home.

549. How much more productive you were at work before e-mail and the Internet.

550. The cruel life lessons that sports impart to kids.

551. People who refuse to see a psychologist because "I don't need to pay someone to help me figure out my issues," but will gladly spend $100 a week at a tanning salon.

552. What most telescopes are really used for.

553. That the U.S. Postal Service began issuing stamps in 1847 yet only recently figured out how to make them self-adhesive.

554. When your fear of overpacking causes you to underpack.

555. Hysterically checking the places you've already hysterically checked while searching for your wallet.

556. Meek office mates who you later learn have been "playing for keeps" behind the scenes all along.

557. When your situation is so hopeless that the best family and friends can offer for encouragement is "Everything will work itself out."

558. People who encourage their dog to hump humans.

559. When your caller ID reads PRIVATE or OUT OF AREA, causing you to weigh the risk of answering an unwanted call versus the frustration of not knowing who wanted to talk to you.

560. Engaging in an activity that used to bring you great pleasure but now feels foreign and lost forever.

561. That yellow peppers don't receive the credit they deserve.

562. People who use the phrase "in the looks department."

563. That childhood bullies are often successful later in life.

564. When you have to cancel plans because you're sick, but you don't sound sick.

565. Ethnic antagonisms that linger for centuries.

566. Paying a toll to cross a bridge when you know you're going in the wrong direction.

567. That Starbursts don't contain one iota of nutritional value.

568. Never anticipating wealth and never receiving it.

569. Being unable to get out of bed in the morning without promising yourself a warm Krispy Kreme doughnut if you succeed.

570. When your steadfast avoidance of carbs impedes your ability to live a normal life.

571. People who give tangential driving directions (e.g., "Make a left at the school with a red stickball strike zone spray painted on the wall. If you reach the Plainview Diner you've gone too far. They have a wonderful Greek salad.").

572. Remembering what a perfect marriage you thought your parents had when you were a little child.

573. How Hollywood can never capture the sound of someone's nose being broken.

574. Suspecting that someone might have slipped a dirty dish in the dishwasher, forcing you to run it again, even though you're pretty sure you already ran it.

575. Coffee chains that expect you to call a small cup of coffee "tall."

576. Shopping with a bickering couple.

577. When your supervisor asks you to perform an ethically odious task.

578. Fonts in which capital I's and lowercase l's look identical.

579. The gluttonous nature of Internet dating.

580. The ease with which Mickey Mantle leapfrogged other liver transplant applicants who'd waited longer, led less destructive lives, and were more likely to survive the operation.

581. Waking up and thinking, Oh, crap, it's Monday morning. Wait . . . ahhhh—it's Sunday. Oh, no, it *is* Monday.

582. Friends who make a spectacle of themselves solely for the purpose of embarrassing you.

583. When the winding steps of a spiral staircase force you to focus on not breaking an ankle.

584. The huge number of people who have never read Auden, Cummings, Dickinson, or Yeats, but purchased Jewel's book of poetry.

585. When asked to name a weakness during your job interview, you reply: "I have a slight gambling problem that sometimes leads me to theft."

586. IKEA on a Sunday afternoon.

587. Realizing that you are neither left-brained nor right-brained.

588. When your doctor asks you to turn your head and cough as he squeezes your testicles during your hernia examination.

589. The apathetic look your pet gives you when you come home from a long vacation.

590. When your shower has terrifying temperature swings depending on when your neighbors flush their toilets.

591. Fortune cookies that don't predict anything (e.g., "You are a bundle of energy, always on the go!").

592. When your roommate never has the money to pay the bills, all of which are in your name.

593. When a car is about to slam into yours, and you instinctively push your palm into the center of the steering wheel, but the horn never sounds, thanks to the engineer who thought it was better, during an emergency, to search for the little horn symbols.

594. People who get so tense before an ostensibly enjoyable occasion that they make it impossible for themselves, or you, to enjoy it.

595. Slipping on ice with your hands in your pockets.

596. Waking up with your head resting on the shoulder of the stranger sitting next to you on the bus.

597. Not knowing which pile to put your light gray clothing in while separating your laundry.

5 Annoying Things About Being a Waitress at a Trendy Restaurant

—by J.F.

1. When customers on special diets demand that you remove the key ingredient from the chef's specialty.

2. When you're on your way to table 12 and table 10 ask for their bread, not grasping that the kitchen is not between tables 10 and 12, so that it is simply impossible for you, on your return trip past table 10, to miraculously appear with a basket of bread and rosemary-infused olive oil, and then they tip you eight percent.

3. Picky eaters who demand to know every ingredient in every dish on the menu, and then say, "I guess I'll just have the penne with tomato sauce."

4. When, at the end of your eight-hour, on-your-feet shift, you're dying to go home, but there's just one table that absolutely refuses to ask for the check, and all you can think about is your 90-minute commute while they sit there chatting away over their tiramisu and cold coffee.

5. When a very large party have finished their meal and you've entered their bill, only to have them announce, "I'm sorry, but those two over there want a separate bill, I want all my food on my own Amex, those five each want to pay independently, and can we please pay for all the alcohol in cash?"

598. When your husband comes home stinking of gin, rushes past you without a kiss, heads for the bathroom, closes the door, turns on the faucets full blast, and yells out, "You go on to bed, honey. . . . I'm gonna be a while."

599. Realizing that you're completely ignoring the meaning of the words you're reading and wondering how long you've been doing that.

600. That your voice only sounds good to you when you're singing alone.

601. When the person holding the camera can't locate the right button, forcing you to stand with a fake grin frozen on your face. 602. Typographical errors.

603. No matter how thoroughly you heal from the loss of love, you are never completely safe from the sudden sting of a vivid remembrance.

604. Any waiter who asks "How's everything?" more than twice during the course of your meal.

605. Hearing a toilet flush on the other end of the phone.

606. That convenience stores at night are inherently frightening.

607. Wildly uneven cheese distribution within an omelette.

608. That even the softest bicycle seat can become ruthless.

609. Alcoholic workaholics.

610. When your husband's violent temper causes him to be passed up for promotions.

611. Hoping for an enthusiastic response and getting a noncommittal one.

612. When you bring a salad from the local deli back to work and they forgot to give you a plastic fork.

613. In this Academy Award–winning performance, Tom Hanks plays an everyman whose inner strength proves greater than the considerable adversity he faces.

614. Being told *"My* money's in the *bank*, sonny!"*

615. Unable-to-get-out-of-the-way-of-the-loud-ambulance-behind-me-because-of-all-the-traffic-in-front-of-me tension.

616. That most people who take karate lessons won't admit they're doing it so they can kick the crap out of people.

617. When your car is stranded on an Alaskan highway and the only human within 200 miles is a Cro-Magnon man wearing a torn parka who communicates through a series of bizarre grunts and gesticulations.

618. Finding your Mercedes vandalized, and dwelling on the possibility that this misfortune represents some kind of just payback for owning a Mercedes.

619. Fraternity pranks that wind up with someone unconscious.

620. The fact that many old people are forced to live out the remainder of their lives in formerly good neighborhoods.

621. Wondering, as your body dives into the frigid pool, why your friend swore the water "feels wonderful."

622. When the speaker begins the seminar by saying, "By a show of hands, how many of you don't know the difference between a stock and a bond?" and you're the only one with your hand in the air.

623. That murder is the quickest path to fame.

624. People who say "Let's grab some din-din."

625. Wondering how asinine you look as you hold a newspaper over your head because it's drizzling.

626. When a husband and wife share an e-mail address.

627. Responding to small talk at 7:22 A.M.

628. Watching the same three bags cycle through the baggage claim area.

629. People who start fretting about New Year's Eve plans in early November.

630. Lifting, then lowering, then lifting your umbrella to avoid colliding with the other umbrellas— none of which seem to ever move up or down.

631. Wondering to what extent a bad habit of yours has become a vice.

632. The struggle between wanting to express your feelings to someone you like and the risk of scaring them away by revealing too much too soon.

633. Losing the only jacket that ever made you feel cool.

634. When your black cummerbund is indistinguishable from your black tuxedo, causing the people who browse through your wedding album to wonder why you wore your pants so high.

635. An auto mechanic who tells you that it will cost $985 to fix your car and then says "Hey, focus on the positive," and cites an even costlier repair you don't need.

636. Those stupid comedy and tragedy masks that represent the theater.

637. When seeing a homeless man sleeping on a park bench stirs less compassion in you than watching an old dog limp along.

638. That *Saturday Night Fever* was a good movie—perhaps a great one—but it unleashed some very ugly forces, particularly in Brooklyn and Staten Island.

639. Suspecting that the only reason you're engaged to your fiancé is because he vaguely reminds you of your ex-boyfriend.

640. How difficult it is to get a Slinky to descend an entire set of stairs without tumbling into a fierce free fall.

641. How foolish you feel wearing a bib while eating lobster in a restaurant.

642. Sensing that the reason your parents are so adamant about sending you to sleepaway camp or boarding school is because they need a long break from you.

643. When you're waiting on line at the grocery store and a stranger asks if he could cut ahead of you because he only has a few items.

644. Helping a friend move back into your living room.

645. That Kentucky Fried Chicken, lacking the courage to stand up for what it truly is, changed its name to KFC.

646. Wondering "Now what?" after your favorite team has just won the Super Bowl or World Series.

647. Reading a sign, three hours into your hike, that says: IN THE UNLIKELY EVENT THAT A BLACK BEAR ATTACKS, USE EVERYTHING AVAILABLE—INCLUDING YOUR BARE HANDS—TO FIGHT BACK. DO NOT PLAY DEAD!

648. Having difficulty opening the gas tank as you try to fill up your friend's car.

649. That when a white man raises his elbows above a certain imaginary line while dancing, he automatically looks like a dork.

650. On-line pop-up advertisements offering to help you get rid of on-line pop-up advertisements.

651. When the piñata at your five-year-old son's birthday party proves unbreakable.

652. Meeting your teacher's husband at the end-of-the-year picnic and realizing that she is not a villain, but a real person with a family that loves and depends on her.

653. That Foot Locker forces its employees to dress like referees.

654. When you want to make a right on red but can't because there's one car in front of you, which makes a right turn when the light turns green.

655. When you are trying to annoy a friend and do it too well, then feel guilty.

656. People who get on the elevator and see that you've already pushed LOBBY, but still push the button again.

657. People who insist "You mustn't open the refrigerator!" when there's a power outage.

658. Driving to a bar, getting rip-roaring drunk with friends, doing the responsible thing and taking a cab home, and waking up the next morning with no idea where you parked your car the night before.

5 Annoying Things About Being a Female Bartender—*by T.W.*

1. That countless guys try to be witty by pointing to the bottle opener in my waistband and saying, "Some can openers have all the luck."

2. Foreigners who think that nodding their heads is a tip.

3. Groups who order one drink at a time. I don't have time to stand there while you say "Gin and tonic, . . . Hey, Jenny, what do you want? Well, I'm having a gin and tonic. . . . No, it's beer before liquor. . . . Hey, Tommy, what do you guys want?"

4. People who ask for moronic shots like Scooby Snacks, Flaming Lamborghinis, Oatmeal Cookies, Drunken Irish Sailor Teetering on a Peg Leg with an Italian Grandma (or whatever). These drinks are for Friday's, and I don't see any flair on my suspenders.

5. People who think it's cool to order ghetto drinks like Thug Passion (just so you know, it's Hennessy and Alizé—classy!).

659. When the barber pushes your head around while cutting your hair.

660. Songs that appear on movie sound tracks but weren't in the movie.

661. The amount of power complete strangers wield over your life.

662. The disgusting course that conversations about what you'd be willing to endure for a lot of money always take.

663. When a slight change in your date's expression shatters the illusion that he or she may be interested in you.

664. How nerve-racking Air Hockey can be.

665. Bending to pick up the subscription cards that fell out of the magazine you're holding.

666. When Wite-Out leaves a bumpy layer that is difficult to write over.

667. That we're more apt to put a picture of a bird than an African American on American currency.

668. That even when you eat healthy food, such as broccoli, it's served in an unhealthy dish, such as General Tso's Chicken.

669. When someone keeps channel-surfing past the one thing that interests you.

670. A passenger safety pamphlet in an airplane depicting a smiling woman strapping a flotation vest around a little girl's neck.

671. The obligatory 19-minute drum solo at any hippy-dippy outdoor concert.

672. When you're just about to reach the climax of a long story you've been telling to a friend and an ambulance drowns you out.

673. When you say "God bless you" to the person who sneezed and he replies, "It was a cough."

674. Emaciated models and celebrities pushing women toward anorexia.

675. Racist rhetoric spewing from a megaphone.

676. When recalling all the jerks you knew at college forces you to root against your alma mater's basketball team.

677. When your history of meeting the wrong person at the wrong time or the wrong person at the right time causes you to become excited about meeting the right person at the wrong time.

678. The fact that you were supposed to flip your mattress over six years ago.

679. People who can't enjoy a book, movie, song, or travel destination unless it's not popular.

680. People who clip their nails in public.

681. Being unable to relate to woodcut illustrations of Pilgrim women weaving.

682. When Dionne Warwick is the most famous celebrity you've ever met.

683. Carefully unfolding each corner of a beat-up dollar bill before inserting it into a vending machine, only to have it come back again and again and again. And again.

684. Knowing that you chose your abrasive friends.

685. The actual percentage of crab in most crab cakes.

686. Paying three bucks for a cup of soda that's 70 percent ice.

687. That people eat something called "goat cheese."

688. Trying to ignore the sound that keeps you from falling asleep.

689. Knowing that all your dog wants to do is socialize with the other dogs from the neighborhood as you pull his leash and say, "Come Max, *let's go for a jog!*"

690. The anxious interior monologue you experience prior to introducing yourself to a large group (e.g., Hello, I'm Scott Cohen. No. Good afternoon everyone, my name's Scott. No. Hi, I'm Scott.).

691. That people who say "I'll let you go" on the phone really mean "I'm desperate to be rid of you."

692. That the most intense laughter you have usually comes at the least appropriate time.

693. When the fortune-teller says to your wife, "You will have all sorts of adventures with all sorts of men."

694. When a number three pencil is the only writing device available to you.

695. Knowing that an acquaintance is going through a disturbing life experience and that she knows you know, as you continue sharing small talk.

696. Receiving a present you already own.

697. When someone tells you, "I'm surrounded by insane people," and you're the only other person in the room.

698. Knowing that your popcorn-crunching is annoying other people in the movie theater.

699. When your child befriends an obvious juvenile delinquent.

700. Lacking a life outside of eBay.

701. Guests who use your shower and don't towel-dry themselves when they're done, drenching the little rug.

5 Annoying Things About Being a Copy Editor—*by S.T.*

1. That the 487,206th time you look up the word "makeup," it *still* doesn't have a hyphen.

2. That you can spend two months of your life absorbing every tiny scrap of information about raising chickens, and have no memory of the subject a week later.

3. When the author insists that his way is the correct way to spell something, and after protracted arguments you find that he's right.

4. That nobody knows the rules of use of commas with restrictive versus nonrestrictive appositive clauses.

5. When you find a Post-it on the floor that says "Absolutely MUST confirm this," with an arrow pointing to something on the page to which the Post-it was formerly stuck.

702. Having no idea what the digital billboard with a constantly increasing 16-digit number stands for.

703. People who stare at their tennis racket and adjust a few strings after making a bad shot.

704. Being stuck in an angry crowd.

705. That a 26-minute rubbernecking delay is just as likely to be caused by a minor fender bender as by a serious accident in which there's really something worth slowing down to see.

706. Parents who advise their child to marry within their religion "because it's one less thing to fight about."

707. That the majority of restaurant tables you will ever sit at will wobble.

708. That you wouldn't have the faintest idea if your accountant was ripping you off.

709. People who think that soy is the solution to all of their health problems.

710. That most state capitals are second-rate towns that would wither away if their economies weren't propped up by government workers.

711. The near impossibility of leaving a buffet without feeling bloated.

712. Refusing to watch *Jeopardy* because it makes you feel dumb.

713. The process of getting to work.

714. The amount of energy mankind puts into discovering new ice cream flavors.

715. When a stranger observes the peculiar, systematic steps you take to avoid contact with germs in a public bathroom.

716. Hiding your lack of emotional generosity by giving gifts.

717. When you've been to all the tourist attractions in Casper, Wyoming, but have never been to the top of the Sears Tower, despite living your entire life in Chicago.

718. When the groom's poem for the bride rhymes "soul mate" with "jailbait."

719. In this sappy movie, Meg Ryan plays an adorable woman who discovers the true meaning of true love.

720. People who only feel comfortable expressing their needs through innuendo (e.g., "Do you think it's stuffy in here?" instead of "Can you please open the window before I am engulfed by a full-blown anxiety attack?").

721. When you're told that in the first several seconds following the big bang the universe cooled from 1,784,000,000,000 degrees to 1,342,000 degrees, and the most intelligent response you can muster is, "It really cooled a lot."

722. That even the "healthy" nut crunch cereals are fattening.

723. That if higher forms of life have been observing mankind through the Hubble telescope, they haven't shown any willingness to help us avert the apocalypse.

724. Wondering if you are behaving immorally by continuing to enjoy the emotional connection you have with another married person, despite the fact that neither of you would ever allow the relationship to become physical.

725. Not listening when someone tells you her name as you're being introduced, causing you to obsess about whether her name will be repeated, leaving you unable to follow the conversation.

726. People who say "guesstimate."

727. Gone are the days when not having to drink from a "sippy cup" brought great joy, and sleeping in a "big boy bed" filled your nights with wonder.

728. That humans have about 60,000 thoughts per day, 59,998 of which they've thought previously.

729. The large number of factors, most of which are beyond your control, that determine whether you have fun at a party.

730. Documentary reenactments that use cheesy close-ups (e.g., plump fingers wrapped around a whiskey bottle in an Elvis biography).

731. Saying to a dog owner: "Can I pet him? Can I pet her? Can I pet it?"

732. That you yell to your spouse "Get the camera!" when your first child inserts a pretzel into her mouth for the first time, and ask, apathetically, "Should we bring the camera?" when your third child graduates from grade school.

733. When the quotation marks in an e-mail you sent are transformed into inane symbols (e.g., So I say to my family, ж%♪ What is this, some kind of an intervention?Ωâžâžâ and my father responds, 🚓🚓🚓Crystal, we think you've got a problem☺👺™).

734. Camping with someone who is high-maintenance.

735. When *Turns for the Worse, Dewey Decimal Days,* and *The Car Pool Driver* are being considered as titles for your life story.

736. When you break up with someone and their reaction makes you wonder why you didn't do it sooner.

737. The natural aptitude kids have for scratching surfaces.

738. Finishing a book not because you're enjoying it but to prove to yourself that you're not a quitter.

Scott Cohen sells custom-printed, Mylar-laminated index tab dividers for a New Jersey–based company. He lives in New York City. Alone. He can be reached at scott2777@yahoo.com.